WHO ARE YOU, FILIPINO YOUTH?

Messages and Meditations

by

William Henry Scott

New Day Publishers
Quezon City
1989

(Most of these essays were first published as a collection by Tala Publishing Corporation in 1976, and are being re-published, with the addition of "Churches of Silence," upon the request of the author, William Henry Scott.)

CONTENTS

WHO ARE YOU, FILIPINO YOUTH?

(Sermon preached on Youth Sunday, 17 August 1975, in the Cathedral of St. Mary and St. John, Quezon City.)

AS I WAS meditating on what to say to you this morning, I wondered just how Youth Sunday differed from all other Sundays. How does speaking to youth differ from speaking to non-youth? What, in fact, is youth? Are you simply people caught in between one particular birthday and another, or what? Who are you, Filipino Youth?

I happen to live on the campus of the state university, so there are plenty of youth around to whom I could put that question. But none of them are able to answer. So I decided that what I would do this morning is to tell you who I think you are.

To begin with, you are youths. Now, as I see it, youth is not an age group defined by beginning in a certain year of life and ending in another. Rather, I conceive of youth as a stage in the development of a mature human being. Just as the caterpillar goes through the chrysalis stage to emerge from the cocoon a full-fledged butterfly, so children go through the stage of youth to become adults. But I do not think that this stage begins with the end of childhood and ends with the beginning of manhood, for youth seems to be a period when childhood and adulthood overlap. It is more like the period in the tadpole's development when the tadpole has already developed the lungs it will need for survival on land as a toad but still retains its fishlike tail for life underwater. So the human youth partakes of the characteristics of both the child and the adult.

Like adults but unlike children, youths have the use of their reason. Children think that all good things come from their parents or their playmates, for instance, while youths and adults understand that all good things come from God—that all the fertilizer in the world won't make the rice grow if God does not intend it to grow. But like children and unlike adults, youths are free of the responsibilities of earning a living, providing for a family, and carrying the burdens of financial, political and social debts. Adults are often so busy earning livings, raising families and bearing burdens that they forget the true source of all bounty and begin to think they themselves are the creators of their own good fortune. Youths, however, unburdened but reasoning, are able to see such issues with a clarity that will later be obscured by self-interest. We call this peculiar condition of youth "idealism."

Now, the human animal is the only one of God's creatures that goes through a stage called youth. We do not call young carabaos or chickens youths, nor do we speak of "youthful" crocodiles or caterpillars. The period of youth must therefore serve some purpose of specifically human development just as the tadpole period serves a purpose uniquely toadish. What, then, is that unique characteristic that youth prepares for? It is simply this: that human beings are designed for love, for it is pleasing to God to be loved by his human creatures. But love requires the ability not to love—that is, love cannot be ordered or demanded. Human beings, therefore, can—indeed, they must—choose whether to love or not, and to select the fit objects of their love. Youth is the period uniquely fitted by its idealism for making such long-range decisions and lifetime choices.

In your present period of youth, then, you will be making the choices which will determine how you will live the rest of your lives. Most of you will choose the mate who is going to share your life, and many of you will choose the career you will follow. Some of you will choose to serve your people and others will choose to serve themselves; and some will choose to serve other countries or citizens of other countries in this country. Some, alas, will make foolish decisions of one moment or one night that will make wise decisions impossible forever after. And some will choose to make no decisions at all—which, of course, will be itself a decision. But, in any case, if the youth is the right time for making life's decisions, you will be well advised to ask yourself who you are and then make your decisions accordingly and wisely.

Now, you are not only youths—you are *Christian* youths. It would be presumptuous for me to try to define what a Christian is. It would also be unnecessary. For we do not recognize Christians by their definitions but, like trees, by the fruits that they produce. We are always hearing about non-Christians these days who are reportedly better Christians than Christians themselves. On the face of it, this is ridiculous, for a non-Christian cannot be either a good or a bad Christian. But what is meant is that these non-Christians' behavior is more like the behavior expected of Christians than the behavior of many Christians. It is easy to tell what kind of behavior is expected of Christians. It is the behavior of people who love God with all their heart and all their mind and all their strength, and their neighbors like themselves.

Of course, the expectation of such behavior presupposes the human ability to love God. Indeed, that ability is the very earmark of humanity, for, as we say, man is the animal designed for love. Unlike other creatures, men can love women, other men, themselves, or God. For some men, infatuation with God is a case of love at first sight: it bursts forth full-blown on the occasion of some sunrise over a calm sea after a night of terrifying typhoon waves, or of receiving back the life of some loved one from the very brink of the tomb. For others, love for God grows gradually over the years as they become more and more aware of the source of their happiness and joy, or of the fact that a lifetime of sinning and selfishness is rewarded not by a God of Justice but a God of Love. Still others only come to love God after loving their neighbors—for when they recognize their neighbors as brothers and sisters, they also recognize the common father who has created them all. And some men, of course, never fall in love at all.

Conversely, some men only come to love their neighbors like themselves because they love God with all their heart and mind and strength— that is, because they love God they learn to love that which God loves. But these two kinds of love are really only different faces of one true Christian behavior, incidental to the fact that while we cannot see or touch God, we can—and some of us do—see and touch our neighbors. It is only then that we can be recognized as Christians by our behavior—when we do our neighbor no harm and allow no one else to do him any harm, when we rejoice in his joy and cry with his tears, when we cannot eat because he is hungry or sleep because he is oppressed.

But you are not only Christian youth—you are Filipino Christian youth. Unlike other Christian youths, you have your own people, different from all other peoples, your own nation different from all other nations, and your own destiny different from other people's destinies. I suppose this is what is meant by "*isang lahi, isang bansa, isang tadhana.*" This people, this nation, and this destiny is the handiwork of the Creator of all peoples, the Governor of all nations, and the Disposer of all destinies, and we must presume that he is just as pleased with what he has wrought in this archipelago as anywhere else.

As a people, you have your own size and shapes, color and characteristics. It is natural for you to be proud of the image in which God created you, and it would be unnatural—perhaps even blasphemous—to be ashamed of it or to hanker after the color and character of another people. So, too, you have your own nation, as youthful and idealistic as you are yourselves. Now, to be a nation is neither good nor bad in itself, for nationhood is not intrinsically either godly or ungodly. We know that there were times when nations did not yet exist, and we know there will come a time when there will be no nations but only one Kingdom of God on earth as in heaven. But in the times in between in which we live, a people without a sense of nationhood is deprived. Deprivation is a kind of bondage, and bondage is that condition of man which prevents the free choices it is man's nature to make, whether by reason of sin or shame, sickness or starvation, subservience or subjugation. Today, then, in the middle of the twentieth century, nation-building may be considered a godly act. And that godly act is your destiny, Filipino youth. If there are those among you who are considering turning your backs on your people and forsaking your nation a-building, you would be well advised to consider this destiny before joining some other people in some foreign land draining off the cream of youth from neighbor states whom they do not love like themselves.

But you are not only Filipino Christian youth—you are Filipino Christian youth in the year 1975. We are all aware that 1975 is a part of a unique period in Philippine history. We are in a state of national emergency, living under martial law, and constructing a new society. The President of the Republic has declared the purpose of this new construction to be the creation of a society uniquely fitted to the needs and genius of the Filipino people, to replace an old society that was fitted to the needs of a colonial past. This is nothing less than an escape from bondage. Not political bondage, of course, for the Filipino people already live in an independent republic whose sovereignty is recognized by all the member states of the United Nations Organization, but spiritual bondage. By "spiritual bondage" I mean that bondage which prevents men from recognizing their own worth in God's eyes and from enjoying the self-confidence which this vision entails. It is the bondage we read about in Holy Scripture when God commands, "Set my people free" and then sends his only Son to do so. If the Filipino people choose to obey this command and seek that reward, it will be your generation that will be the keystone of the newly constructed Filipino nation.

For you are different from all Filipinos in the past, and there will never be Filipinos like you again in the future. You are the first generation of Filipino citizens to be born and raised in an independent republic. Your parents and grandparents were born and raised in a foreign colony, and your children and grandchildren will be born and raised in the nation which you decide to create in your own lifetime. Your parents, if they were good citizens of the colonial society in which they lived, and learned their lessons well, absorbed the ideals of another people and accepted the value judgments of a foreign regime. But you, born and raised in a sovereign state, can seek out those values which will enable your people and your nation to find and follow their destiny as an independent republic. Yet it is clear that your efforts and energies as you labor at this task are still frustrated by the scars of those colonial shackles which were actually struck off before you were even born.

This, then, is the peculiar dilemma in which you find yourselves as Filipino Christian youth in the year of our Lord nineteen hundred and seventy-five.

But you are not only in 1975—you are at a particular day in 1975 —the twelfth Sunday after Trinity. Now, the twelfth Sunday after Trinity has been set aside and marked as Youth Sunday in the Central Diocese of the Philippine Episcopal Church. And the portion of the Good News appointed to be proclaimed aloud on this day you have already heard this morning. It is the well-known and thought-provoking story in the Gospel according to St. Mark of the deaf man with an impediment in his speech who was brought to our Lord to be healed by faith. Our Lord placed his fingers in the man's ears and on his tongue and looked up to heaven and said, *Ephphata*—that is, "Be opened!"—and the man's ears were opened and his tongue was loosed.

Does this story contain a message for Filipino youth today? Is it possible that the reason Filipino youth neither hears nor responds to the voice of Christ calling the Filipino people out of bondage is that they are deaf and dumb? Perhaps Filipino youth speaks with an impediment because they are made to speak in the language of another people, a language which cannot express the nuances of their frustration and which lacks the vocabulary to define the anguish of their people. Perhaps Filipino youth is deaf because their ears are stopped with the discordant din of foreign advice in the confessional, foreign music in the movie houses and foreign firearms on the field of battle.

Filipino youth, will you not be cured of this affliction? Will you not come to Him who loves the Filipino people better than they can love themselves, and let Him put His fingers in your ears and on your tongue that your hearing might be restored and your tongue loosened so that you speak out straight and clear?

Ephphata, Filipino youth, be opened!

A FRAME OF MIND FOR CHURCH AND YOUTH

(Address delivered at the inauguration of the Cathedral Youth Center, 277 E. Rodriguez, Sr., Blvd., 24 October 1971.)

IF I SEEM a little nervous this morning, it's because I secretly suspect I was invited here by mistake. What I think happened is that the Chairman of the Program Committee of the Cathedral Youth Organization didn't really know who I was, but he read my name in the *Baguio Midland Courier* where a naughty friend of mine referred to me in her column as an "Igorot student activist." And then when he learned the truth that I was really over thirty and not under thirty, he was too polite to take back the invitation. At any rate, here I am, and having got this far, I will go ahead.

Of course, there is also the other possibility. There is the possibility the Chairman really knew who I was but decided to invite me anyway. This would be very flattering, because I notice these days that members of the Now generation don't often want to listen to a talk by a member of the Has-Been generation. Seriously, though, it is an honor, and I know it, and I thank you for it.

The invitation I received said, Please feel free to choose any topic you wish. But—the Cathedral Youth suggests that you could speak on the importance of the Youth Center on the Church's ministry to the youth in relation to their Christian development as good citizens of the Church and of the Philippines. It sounds more like a doctoral dissertation than a twenty-minute talk, but God being my helper and you being patient, I will try.

I should admit first off that when I received the invitation, I didn't even know what the Youth Center was. So I asked the Chairman, "What is the Youth Center? I mean, is it a building, or a program, or just a frame of mind?" And he replied, "Yes, a frame of mind."

Of course, we were both joking. What he meant was that the second story had not yet been built on this Cathedral Hall, but that everybody hoped it would be. But actually, I like that expression, "a frame of mind." What I think the importance of the Youth Center is to be a kind of frame of mind.

Of course, even a frame of mind needs some kind of physical support, so the Youth Center will also have to have some sort of material foundation. Our youth will need shade from the sun and shelter from the rain if they want to spend their idle moments meeting old friends and making new ones. Many of our youth are lonely in this large impersonal city, especially those far away from home or, worse yet, strangers for a time in their own home, so our Youth Center should provide the opportunity, unprogrammed and unpretentious, to meet others like themselves. Many of our youth are bored, and in their boredom engage in activities of the moment or for an afternoon or a night which they and their families and townmates will regret all the rest of their lives, so our Youth Center should provide games and reading matter to help dispel that boredom. But an even worse affliction of youth is frustration, for boredom is caused by lack of inner resources and little thinking, while frustration is caused by a wealth of inner resources that find no outlet, and a great deal of thinking. It will take nothing less than a frame of mind to suggest the outlets to assuage this frustration.

As I understand, one of the purposes of this inauguration this morning is to provide an occasion for receiving donations toward the initial establishment of the physical foundation which our Youth Center will need. I see that some chessboards and checker sets have already been donated, so I hope you will permit me to make this donation of a year's subscription to the *Asian Philippine Leader* magazine.

I take a small pleasure in making this donation, but what a large pleasure I would take if all the problems of Filipino youth could be solved by some American reaching in his pocket and pulling out a checkbook! But it is not so simple as all that, is it? As I look around, I see many faces missing. I see many young Filipinos, young members of the Episcopal Church who are not here with us. I wonder where they are, and what they are doing. Do you suppose they are someplace else reading a newspaper? Or playing chess or checkers? No, I don't think so. I don't think they left the Church because the Church did not provide them with enough magazines or chessboards. I think they left the Church because they, in their frame of mind, were asking questions which the Church in its frame of mind wasn't answering. And I think the Church in its frame of mind was answering questions nobody was asking in any frame of mind.

Now, you will notice that I have been referring to Youth and Church as if they were two different things separate from one another. This is a fallacy, of course. I made this fallacy deliberately because it is a common error and I thought that by repeating the common error I could make the correction more forcefully. For Youth is part of the Church, is it not? And its frame of mind ought to be part of the frame of mind of the Church as a whole.

If I understand what Filipino Youth is saying, you do not ask to be the whole Church, or to run the Church, or to dictate to the Church. You want to be a part of the Church—a responsible, active, and influential part. You want to inform, reform, and form the Church together with whatever parts are not Filipino Youth. And that is why I think our Youth Center should be a kind of workshop for informing, reforming, and forming the Church's frame of mind.

Now, how do we go about making a frame of mind? Well, the best way is by phrasing questions and then seeking answers to them. This, in other words, is simply the search for truth. I think, five or ten years ago, I would not have mentioned this because it seemed to me then that what many Filipino youths meant by the search for truth was finding the right answer to pass the exam so they could earn a degree and get a job and live happily and selfishly ever after. But no more. Today, fortunately, Filipino youth is seeking the truth, actively and aggressively.

Now, the best way to ask questions and find answers is by the exchange of ideas. From this it follows that if people who have the same ideas exchange them, nothing will be learned. But if people whose ideas are very different exchange them, much may be learned. So, the more unlike the positions of the people who exchange the ideas, the more there is to be learned, though this is not guaranteed.

After exchanging ideas with other people, we may conclude that our own ideas are wrong, and therefore be able to change them more readily. Or we may conclude that our ideas were right in the first place and so understand them better and be more willing to die for them.

Such an exchange of ideas, of course, requires an ecumenical atmosphere. Fortunately, we live in an ecumenical age. Our Church, our Cathedral, this Youth Center are all formally committed to an ecumenical spirit. The invitations that brought some of you here this morning said that all youths would be welcome whatever their church affiliations. Perhaps this invitation should have been extended to read, "whatever their church affiliations, *if any*." For many youths with ideas ready for exchange have no church affiliation at all or only a pretended affiliation for other purposes. For Christian youth is being called upon to answer important questions which non-Christians are asking, and non-Christians are answering important questions which Christian youth is asking.

What are some of these important questions?

Well, probably the most important question which is being asked, not only by Filipino youth but by Christians all over the world, is this: "Does Christ pass judgment on society?" And for those who answer this question "Yes," there inevitably follows a second question: "Has Christ passed judgment on this society?" And to those who answer the second question "Yes," there inevitably follows a third question: "Is Christ calling me to change this society?" And to those who answer "Yes" to the third question, there inevitably follows a fourth question, and it is the most important question of all: "Will Christ pass judgment on the new society?"

Now, these are questions which it takes courage to ask and to answer. Fortunately, Filipino youth has courage. For the different questions require different kinds of courage. The first three—"Does Christ pass judgment on society?" "Has Christ passed judgment on this society?" and "Is Christ calling me to change this society?"—can all be asked and answered in the streets. And it takes courage to go into the streets. But the fourth question, the most important one of all—"Will Christ pass judgment on the new society?"—cannot be asked or answered in the streets. It can only be asked and answered among yourselves, in a group meeting like this, in the honest and courageous exchange of ideas. And that requires an even greater kind of courage. For it it requires courage to contradict your enemies, how much more courage it requires to contradict your friends, your companions, your classmates. Who is there among you who will deny, if he is honest, that it takes more courage to speak out against the popular opinion of a strong leader in your own age group than to man the barricades?

I know this from an experience in my own youth—though you may not believe there ever was such a time. I was a dormitorian in a boy's school, and, like all dormitorians, we boys used to play tricks on the master-in-charge, tricks which we considered a kind of just punishment for his abuse of power. One time we decided to play the following trick. In the middle of the night, we would go outside his room and apply fire to the brass doorknob on his door so that the heat would pass through the door and make the brass doorknob on the inside hot, too. Then, when it was red-hot, we would ring the doorbell and run away, and when he got up and went to the door all sleepy, he would grab the doorknob and burn his hand. Now it took courage to do this. So, when we were planning it, we quickly discovered who among us had courage and who did not. The brave ones wanted to do it and did do it, and the bravest of all was the one who applied the fire to the doorknob. And those of us who were afraid to do it were divided into the little cowards and the big cowards. The little cowards were those who wanted to do it but were afraid to do it because they feared getting caught. The big cowards—and I was one of them—were those who thought it was wrong to do it but *didn't have the courage to say so.*

I will confess that I have been haunted for thirty-five years by the memory of that act of cowardice. Because, in the first place, the trick was a complete failure as far as teaching the master-in-charge a lesson was concerned. For you don't change a man's ideas by burning his hand. But worse than that, I came to realize that when we were talking about justice and injustice, what we really meant was just plain hatred.

For the past few years, I have been hearing Filipino youth talking a lot about social justice and injustice, and the memory of that story keeps coming back to me. At first I thought it was the same case all over again because all I saw was violence and destruction. But slowly I came to see that Filipino youth really meant something else by justice. What they really meant was Love. You may think that sounds very funny. Let me show you why I say it.

When the popular press in this country commits an injustice against the President, no youth protests. When one politician commits an injustice against another politician, no youths go out to demonstrate. When a squatter commits an injustice against a landlord, no student takes to the streets. But when the rich and powerful commit an injustice against the poor and help-less, all Filipino youth unites to man the barricades. Is this anything else than Love? Love of fellowmen? Why do rich Filipino youth care whether some other Filipino is weak and miserable, if not for love? Why do well-fed Filipino students find it difficult to swallow their food in the presence of the starving, if not for love? And if you have not learned this in your own life, we have the example of the Gospel story ready at hand, for did not God himself take on flesh and walk among us so He could feel our pain and share our suffering?

Of course, it is difficult really to picture our Lord as a flesh-and-blood man who probably caught cold and got sore feet when he walked for four-and-a-half hours in the rain just like any other youth. Yet, is it not as Shakespeare said of another Jew, "If you tickle him, does he not laugh? If you prick him, does he not bleed?" And if he had the feelings of a man, did he not have the sympathies of a man? I was thinking about this one day a few weeks ago when I was more than ordinarily depressed by the deliberate, man-made tragedies which happen every day in this only Christian nation in Asia, and I said to Father Hibbs, "Do you suppose that when our Lord was on earth and he opened the morning newspaper and read the kind of news I read this morn-ing, he got a little sick to his stomach?" And Father Hibbs replied, "Well, I think the answer to that is in the shortest verse in the Bible." Now, I never graduated from a theological seminary, but I do know what the shortest verse in the Bible is. "Jesus wept."

But the real significance of Father Hibbs's answer was not in the mere fact that Jesus wept. It was the occasion of his weeping. For Jesus did not weep when he was arrested and unjustly accused of subversion. Jesus did not weep when he was subjected to third-degree treatment in a Roman stockade. No, Jesus did not weep for himself. He wept in sympathy for the sorrow of a friend bereft of a loved one. And if he wept for the sorrow of one friend, would he ever have had time to dry his eyes if he lived in the world in which we live?

It is so difficult to take a question like that seriously that I would like to invent a kind of parable to illustrate better what I mean. I think I am in good tradition in doing this: our Lord himself told parables to illustrate his points, and so do preachers in the pulpit in our Cathedral almost every Sunday. Let me pretend there is a fifth Gospel, intended to speak to our society in our time as the other four were intended to speak to another society in other times. Let me pretend that this Gospel has some such title as "The Good News of our Lord and Saviour Jesus Christ—How He Came to Visit the Philippine Archipelago from Aparri to Jolo." And let me pretend that I open this Gospel to any page at random, and read verses like this:

And lo, it came to pass that Jesus went forth from the boat and set his foot on the shore of the Lake of Lanao, and he saw how the people of that land were in conflict, contending with one another, and even the latchet of his sandal was wet with Filipino blood. And Jesus wept.

And he passed into the highest mountains of northern Luzon, and he saw how the people of those highlands were in conflict, neighbor contending against neighbor, beating their plowshares into swords. And Jesus wept.

And he descended to the green coastal plain along the South China Sea, and he saw how the people of that land were in conflict, and how their leaders had profaned his temple by shedding human blood. And Jesus wept.

And he passed through the great and good valley of the Cagayan River and he saw how the people of that land were in conflict, and risen up in armed rebellion, brother against brother, son against father, daughter against mother. And Jesus wept.

And he passed into the great halls of learning of the capital city of that country, and he saw how the Filipino studentry was prostrate with discouragement, their hearts melted like wax. And Jesus wept.

And he entered into the barrooms and brothels of that greater metropolitan district and sat down with harlots and Filipino youths, and he saw how they were devouring themselves with riotous living because they had lost all hope and all faith. And Jesus wept.

And he passed over the cloverleaf in the city called Caloocan, and through the Plaza Miranda, and across the bridge called Mendiola, and he saw how the citizens of the country were shooting their sons and daughters like birds. And Jesus wept.

And he was invited to a wedding feast in the greatest hotel in that city, and he sat down to a banquet so sumptuous it might readily have fed every sacada from Tarlac to Dumaguete City. And Jesus wept.

And then passing through locked doors, he entered into the secret chambers of the most highly placed of that land—and he saw how the money-changers were changing the money. And Jesus wept.

And then, at the last, passing along the Espana Extension, he entered into Cathedral Heights to join with us this morning in the celebration of the inauguration of that youth center that shall be raised in his Name for the purpose of bringing closer to him the young people of his Church and the young citizens of the republic. For, believe me, Filipino youth, he is here in our midst just as surely as I am standing here before you, and he is looking at you and looking at me with the tears still wet on his cheeks, and he is asking, "Young friend, what do you say to all of this? Little comrade, what are you going to do about it?"

For me, I can only sincerely hope and devoutly pray that, with his Grace and your courage, this youth center will become the anvil on which Filipino youth will beat out Christian answers to these questions.

A MEDITATION ON THE GREENING
OF CATHEDRAL HEIGHTS

(A meditation given in the chapel of St. Andrew's Theological Seminary at the Vigil of the Annunciation, 24 March 1972.)

YOU ARE at the end of a school year, in the midst of your Lenten discipline, and at the beginning of the new summer assignments where you will enjoy more intimate contacts with the Filipino people than are possible in this institution. It is fitting for the purpose of meditation to bring these three time facets of your immediate life together so that in your present meditation you can prepare for your future assignment by thinking about the past school year. As an historian, I am aware that this past year has been a year of change, bringing to fruition some of the changes begun over the past several years. As a Christian, I consider these changes for the most part good. I like to think of them as "the greening of Cathedral Heights," taking that term from the title of a recent book by Charles A. Reich, *The Greening of America*, which tells the story of the impact of youth on modern American society. It is a thought-provoking title with a good literary ring, and, I submit, entirely appropriate for the changes which have been taking place around us.

To begin this meditation I would like to focus your attention on the immediate environment in which you live. I am sure that when you came in off the busy streets of Manila for the first time, all of you were struck by the atmosphere of elegant privacy of these immaculate white buildings scattered along tree-shaded roads winding past sunken gardens with delicate fountains playing into artificial fish ponds. To some of you, it may have appeared to be a haven of quiet Christian order in a noisy, grasping world; to others of you, it may have seemed more like a symbol of the Church's withdrawal from a sick and suffering society. But in either case, you can sharpen the image by recalling what your life used to be like in this very institution back before these changes took place.

Those of you who have been here long enough will remember how you used to spend most of your time in starchy white cassocks answering a series of bells which told you when to rise, bathe, sleep, eat, pray, play, work, study, attend classes and go to bed—although I suppose that from bedtime till dawn you were thrown on your own resources. These regulations were intended to develop a lifelong priestly character in the older ones among you and guard the younger ones just in from the provinces against the distractions and temptations of the greater metropolitan district. You were honor-bound not to leave the premises without permission and to be in uniform when you did; you agreed not to marry before graduation, and it was hoped that entangling alliances would be prevented by the steel louvres on the dormitory windows facing the school of nursing. Your confidence in the wisdom of the alien theologians who operated the institution and your gratitude for a free education at foreign expense dampened whatever doubts or dissent might otherwise have arisen. It was a way of life which required little responsibility on your part, provided little opportunity for decision-making, and placed a high premium on conformity. And that is just what it looked like.

This appearance began to change with the coming of Trinity College. A hundred flowers now started to bloom amidst the poured concrete and asphalt paths as boys and girls together chatted on the chapel steps, perched in the low-hanging branches of mango trees to cram for exams, or relaxed in the cool cathedral shade to take notes between classes. Coeds in skirts shorter than their hair began to borrow books from your library, and you yourselves began to sit down in the rainbow-colored ranks of your Trinity classmates as St. Andrew's joined the Philippine educational system for the first time. Regulations relaxed, compulsory attendance was minimized, and eventually even postulants bloomed out in the bright-colored shirts and shoulder-length hair which are the proud marks of male independence on all the campuses of the free world today.

So the greening began.

But that greening was only the outward sign of an inward quickening of the spirit. The perceptive ones among you began to realize that the huge sums of money spent on Cathedral Heights had not been invested simply to buy books for you to press your noses into, but rather to provide the incentives for potential leaders to look up from the printed page, cast a newly enlightened eye on the world about them, and apply the lessons they had learned. What had been interpreted as your dependence on parents and scholarships for support was now seen to be a kind of independence from the network of social, political, and financial debts which prevent people of my generation from following the dictates of our own conscience to achieve our finer ideals. So a concerned minority began to sit up, take notice, and involve itself. Thinkers among you began to make their thoughts public, dissenters stiffened their spines, spread their feet apart, and squared their shoulders, and radicals took up bullhorns and paintpots to protest what they considered the complacency of contemporary society in an evil world. It was probably inevitable that you would leave these Heights and take to the streets of Manila when the writ of *habeas corpus* was suspended and demand the restoration of civil liberty at the very gates of the presidential palace, or to hike through four hours of rain to close ranks with an outraged Filipino public when goonish citizens of Caloocan cut down peaceful student demonstrators in cold blood in broad daylight. So, too, when a crowd of thousands assembled in front of Congress in unambiguous concern for the state of the nation during the President's opening address, you were standing there to be counted with the blood-red banner of St. Andrew the Martyr flying bravely overhead beside a dozen others of like hue.

The past year also saw the 54th Convention of the Philippine Episcopal Church here on Cathedral Heights. In historic fact, this was the first convocation since the division of the old missionary district into three dioceses. But it will probably go down in history as the first convocation since the Greening of Cathedral Heights. It was scarcely ten minutes old when an unsigned resolution reached the floor where it was promptly sponsored by an archdeacon of the Church: it moved the seating of youth delegates and was immediately supported by no less an eminence than the Chancellor of the Church and Parliamentarian of Convocation. As it was unanimously passed, the resolution charged each diocesan bishop to produce two delegates of youth at the next annual convocation, and instructed the Committee on Constitution and Canons to study means for adding one youth to the permanent membership of National Council. Next, the oldest delegate present read a position paper prepared by one of your young people's organizations which eloquently stated the distressing events transpiring at that very moment in our own St. Luke's Hospital in connection with an attempt to unionize the workers, and it electrified the assembly with word that five student chaplains had been threatened with Metrocom arrest and so-called "invitation" to Camp Crame. Since the Hospital Administrator never appeared to present his side of the case, the younger generation made its moral point as the issue dragged on into heated debate during the last hour of the final session, and moved many delegates who might otherwise have been lobbying for more selfish local benefits to take a good hard look at the Church's corporate conscience instead. So you youths dominated the Church convoked not by grabbing microphones or disrupting proceedings but simply by sitting quiet and watchful in the back of the hall, your steady gaze fixed on the behavior of another generation.

Since Convocation, observant residents have had a new awareness of your verdant presence here. By day the majority of you tread these broad lawns with pride and sense of belonging; by night a concerned minority of you gather in offices and halls with your fellows from other schools and churches to consider your country's ills. While some boyish adolescents among you are sneaking out to barrooms in hopes of becoming men overnight, real men among you are cutting chapel and curfew to answer more compelling calls to service. For this fresh wind passing over Cathedral Heights is actually blowing in from the Republic of the Philippines. The babble of Filipino voices now breaking the alien silence of the Cathedral Hall since it has become a youth center echoes a new sense of community, nationhood and sovereignty. It is no coincidence that when thugs threatened the lives of two of you who had helped hospital workers organize, one of you was an Igorot Anglican and the other a lowland Aglipayan. It is this quickening spirit which has given some of you the confidence to lean casually against the nerve center of the two Philippine churches and fiscalize the Filipino conscience. For it is you young lovers of the whole Filipino people who are teaching public officials and church magnates alike to walk with more careful tread down a narrower and straighter path than they have ever trod before.

Well, I have tried to focus a few images for your inner eye which I hoped would raise questions that might lead you to seek a new life, a life in which much responsibility would be required of you, many opportunities would be provided for decision-making, and a low premium would be placed on conformity. First, I tried to frame a small picture of your immediate environment; then, the picture of that larger environment of which the smaller is rapidly becoming a part; and finally the conduct of some of you as you responded to this change. For, after all, is not each Lenten Season a kind of gateway through which we are beckoned to a new life, to new duties, new service, and a new awareness of our own worth in God's eyes? And so I would like to leave with you just one more image—the changing image of youth, the image of you yourselves.

Back before the Greening, people of my generation used to cherish a picture of you future leaders of the Philippine Independent and Episcopal Churches as a kind of tender plants growing in a seedbed; we thought it was our job to keep the mud in that seedbed soft and squishy, to regulate the level of the water, and to dump fertilizer in on you when needed. But now the picture is clearer. Now it can be seen that you are not seedlings growing in the mud at all. Instead, you are growing in a crack in a rock, a rock of stony indifference and ungodly injustice. Perhaps during forty days and forty nights of meditation, Satan in the wilderness or in the garden has tried to persuade you that this crack in that rock is a safe and secure place to grow. Never mind that you will be squeezed and pinched and unable to achieve your full maturity—at least you will be protected from having to answer the call of a Master whose service may require you to drink from a bitter cup which he will not let pass from your lips.

But listen to me, my young Christian comrades. I tell you that if you want to, you can split that rock wide open! You can send forth your roots to grow all over that rock, so that, thus firmly planted and firmly fixed, you grow up straight and tall and spread out your branches by acres and hectares until they bend down heavy with fruit, Filipino fruit, and touch the ground from Aparri to Jolo! And it may be that I, and others of my generation, will not live to enjoy the shade of that tree, but he who planted the tree and he who makes it grow, he loves it, and when it bears he will taste of the fruit and the flavor, ah, the flavor, believe me, *will be sweeter than the honeycomb in his mouth!*

SHOWING FORTH GOD'S LOVE
IN AN UNLOVING WORLD

(Sermon preached at the installation of the Rev. Luke Alaban as pastor of the United Church of Christ in the Philippines, Cubao, Quezon City, 24 September 1972. Readings: Jeremiah 1:9-10; Matthew 10:16-22.)

MY CHRISTIAN brother Luke, you are called here this morning, in this particular moment of the unfolding of God's mysterious plan for his people in the Philippines, to lead this congregation to show forth God's love in an unloving world.

The love of God is very different from the love of man. I suppose all men love their parents and their children and themselves. But if you love only those who love you, what reward have you? Do not even the tax collectors do the same? Indeed, does not even the she-wolf do the same, loving the wolfling in her own wolfish way? But the love of God is not like that. For God loves all his children and all men are his children, though their number passes under-standing.

The love of God may be likened to the love of a certain father who had eight sons. Now the eighth son happened to fall ill and came near to death, so the father left the seven to care for the one. Then four fell on hard times and lost their living and their sustenance, so the father sold all that he had and went to succor the four. Then seven came into evil days and became destitute and miserable, saving only the eldest, who prospered and became a great lord and wealthy man in his place. So the father went to his firstborn son and asked for help for the seven, but he would not give anything out of his estate. And the father said, "Oh, you wicked son! Did I not give you all that you had and now you will not spare a single penny for these your brothers who are destitute and miserable?" Now, tell me, Brother Luke, how will that father show his love to all eight of his sons?

It is like the hard sayings of our Lord, Luke—a difficult question. But it is one which you and your congregation will be called on to answer. For we live in a world which is like that father's family, a world in which seven out of eight of God's children are destitute and miserable—sick or hungry, poor or undernourished .Their knowledge of love is limited to the natural affections of their wives and children; they will never understand the love of a God who makes his sun to rise on the evil and on the good, and sends rain on the just and on the unjust. If they are lucky, they may hear the message of God's love proclaimed from the pulpit, but they will probably never experience it at the hands of those few whom God has chosen to be the stewards of his goods in this world. And if they are luckier still, they will go to school and learn that God endowed them with the inalienable rights of life, liberty and the pursuit of happiness. But liberty and happiness they will never know, and life they will purchase only at the price of a usury that will reduce them to a bitter penury which they will pass on to their children like a communicable disease.

These are the unlovely facts of the world into which God calls us to love the unloved in the unlovable little places where we find them, Brother Luke. Perhaps that is why he calls forth his servants not with words of love but with such stern commands as he gave your predecessor, Jeremiah, when he put forth his hand and touched his lips and said:

> Behold, I have put my words in your mouth. See, I have set you this day over nations and over kingdoms, to pluck up and to break down, to destroy and to overthrow, to build and to plant.

These are strong words: they fall harsh on the ear and heavy on the conscience, and we do not find "love" among them. How then are we to understand them as God's command to show forth his love in an unloving world?

Perhaps we can think of them as the words of a certain king who planted a beautiful garden in all the world. And when it was finished, he saw that it was good, and he loved every plant that was in it. But a rich man came and planted a fruit tree in the center of the garden. And the fruit tree grew and flourished and sent out its roots into every corner of the garden and sucked up all the water so no other plant could drink or grow; and it spread out its branches and leaves until they blotted out all the light of the sun so that no other plant could know God's goodness. And when the time was ripe, the rich man came and gathered up all the fruit unto himself and stored it in his barns so that there was no harvest for any other man. Now, when the king who owns the garden will come and see what has happened to it, what will he do? How say you, Brother Luke, will he not call forth his good gardener, Jeremiah, and send him into the garden to pluck up and break down until he restores that garden to its original beauty and bounty?

Of course, you know all this better than I do, my Christian brother, because you are not just beginning your ministry in this unloving world. You have already made love to the unloved by sharing their unlovable little corner of the world in Zone One, Tondo. You tried to pluck up and break down the barriers that prevented that barren garden from yielding fruit for all God's children living there. And you were misunderstood, persecuted and expelled from one Christian institution for trying to show forth God's love to the least of his sons and daughters working there. No, this is not the beginning of your ministry. For yesterday you were alone, but today you are united with this congregation of Christian comrades who will love and support you as you both go forth into the world with common courage and commitment. You are not called here to serve them, but rather to lead them as you and they go out from this place together on your common mission of service to those who need most to be served in this land.

And I tell you, Christian friend, it is a mission which calls for even more commitment and courage this morning than yesterday morning. For this morning, all of us are apprehensive and some of us are afraid, and when men are apprehensive and afraid, they are likely to think of their own safety and comfort before their neighbors' needs. Yet we do so at our peril, for the unloved need our love even more now than before, and there is one higher authority who is judge of all men who will weigh those of us who love ourselves more than our neighbors and find us wanting. He is that same Lord of all history who could foresee today's events when he commissioned the first twelve of your fellows in Galilee, Pastor Alaban. Listen again how he calls you:

Behold, I send you out as sheep in the midst of wolves' so be wise as serpents and innocent as doves. Beware of men; for they will deliver you up to councils, and flog you in their synagogues, and you will be dragged before governors and kings for my sake, to bear testimony before them and the Gentiles. When they deliver you up, do not be anxious how you are to speak or what you are to say; for what you are to say will be given to you in that hour; for it is not you who speak, but the Spirit of your Father speaking through you. Brother will deliver up brother to death, and the father his child, and children will rise against parents and have them put to death; and you will be hated by all for my name's sake. But he who endures to the end will be saved.

So take heart, Brother Luke; he who asks of no man more than he can give will not send you out into an unloving world to show forth his love alone. No, he will send you out shoulder to shoulder with the company of his chosen people assembled here this morning—those who have been chosen to be fed while others are hungry, to be clothed while others are naked, healthy while others are sickly, celebrating while others are dying—and free while others are in prison.

A PEOPLE CHOSEN BY GOD

(Sermon preached at the Ordination of the Reverend Ignacio Soliba to the Priesthood in the Church of St. Mary the Virgin, Sagada, Mountain Province, on 4 February 1974.)

THERE WAS a people chosen by God.

They were a weak and humble people, living far from the routes of commerce and the paths of empire. They had no kings or kingdoms, no palaces or temples, nor even any history. They were surrounded by great and ancient armies. But God did not choose those great countries for his people; instead, he chose these like orphans out of the wilderness. He chose them to be the instruments of his plan for this world and the salvation of his whole creation. And he promised that he would make them a great and prosperous people if they would obey his laws.

But they did not understand God's plan. They thought the purpose of his covenant was to make them a great and prosperous people. So when God commanded them, "Thou shalt not kill," they obeyed because it was good for business. But when he ordered them, "You shall not exact interest if you lend money to any of my people with you who is poor," they disobeyed because it was bad for business. They began to lord it over each other to become great and prosperous, and built big houses fit for kings. So God raised up a prophet in their midst to warn them.

> Woe to him who builds his house by unrighteousness, and his upper rooms by injustice; who makes his neighbor to serve him for nothing, and does not give him his wages, and says, "I will build myself a great house with spacious upper rooms," and cuts windows for it, panelling it with cedar, and painting it with vermillion. Do you think you are a king because you compete in cedar?

Now, when they saw that God was angry, his chosen people said, "Let us go up to his house and worship him. Six days we will work for ourselves but the seventh we will set aside for him." So six days they did what they pleased, but on the seventh they went up to his temple and fell down before him. They sang praises to his name and burned incense in his honor, and humbled themselves with sackcloth and ashes and fasted. But God was not deceived, and he said to them:

Behold, in the very day of your fasting you seek your own pleasure, and oppress all your workers. Behold, you fast only to quarrel and to hit with your wicked fist. Fasting like yours this day will not make your voice to be heard on high. Is this the fast that I choose? Is not this the fast that I choose: to loose the bonds of wickedness, to undo the thongs of the yoke, to let the oppressed go free, and to break every bond? Is it not to share your bread with the hungry, and bring the homeless poor into your house; when you see him naked, to cover him? Then shall your light break forth like the dawn, and your healing spring speedily forth; your righteousness shall go before you and the glory of the Lord shall be your rear guard. Then you shall call, and the Lord will answer; you shall cry, and he will say, Here I am.

So God raised up kings to set over them like shepherds, to lead them in the right way and to protect the weak against the strong. But their kings were more selfish than the rest, so that their last condition was worse than the first. So God called out to them in his anger and said:

Ho, shepherds of Israel, who have been feeding yourselves! Should not shepherds feed their sheep? You eat the fat, you clothe yourselves with wool, you slaughter the fatlings; but you do not feed the sheep. The weak you have not strengthened, the sick you have not healed, the crippled you have not bound up, the strayed you have not sought, and with force and harshness you have ruled them.

And so God decided to punish them. He called up kings and conquerors as his servants from the countries round about to oppress and afflict them. But from their very oppressors they learned new ways to disobey God's law. And when God saw it, he could bear his wrath no longer, and his heart turned stony cold within him, and he swore:

This is Jerusalem; I have set her in the center of the nations, with countries round about her. And she has wickedly rebelled against my ordinances more than the nations, and against my statutes more than the countries round about her, by rejecting my ordinances and not walking in my statutes. Therefore, thus says the Lord God, Behold, I, even I, am against you; and I will execute judgments in the midst of you in the sight of the nations. And because of all your abominations I will do with you what I have never yet done, and the like of which I will never do again.

But then, God's wrath enduring but the twinkling of an eye, he remembered how they were his children, and he loved them. And when he saw how they were so afflicted, his heart melted again within him, and he regretted what he had done, and he said, No,

I will make with them a covenant of peace and banish wild beasts from the land, so that they may dwell securely in the wilderness and sleep in the woods. And I will make them and the places round about my hill a blessing. And the trees of the field shall yield their fruit, and the earth shall yield its increase, and they shall be secure in their land. And they shall know that I am the Lord, when I break the bars of their yoke, and deliver them from the hand of those who enslaved them. They shall no more be a prey to the nations, nor shall the beasts of the land devour them; they shall dwell securely and none shall make them afraid. And I will provide for them prosperous plantations so that they shall no more be consumed with hunger in the land, and no longer suffer the reproach of the nations.

That people is the Filipino people.

For when God decided to raise up one Christian nation in Asia to announce his plan for this half of the world, he did not choose a great nation or an ancient empire. Instead, he chose a weak and humble people cut off from the mainstreams of empire like orphans in a watery desert. He selected a people without Great Walls or Taj Mahals or Borobudurs or Angkor Wats, a race without princes, palaces or the prerogatives of power. He chose them to be the instrument of his will, and compassed them round about with great nations and mighty empires, and conquerors and oppressors to water their soil with blood to prepare the seedbed for a New Jerusalem in a New Asia.

So we, here today, in this New Society, in this province, in this community, may read the signs of the times in the history of the Children of Israel of old. Like them, we stand in danger of the same error and the same punishment—to think that God's purpose is to set us up as a great and prosperous people over others. But we need not. For God sent his very Son to summarize the laws of his Covenant so simply and so clearly that we cannot mistake them unless we wish to.

You shall love the Lord your God with all your heart and your soul and your mind. This is the first and great commandment, and the second is like unto it, you shall love your neighbor as yourself.

Now, we are men of good will and not kings or conquerors, and we do not oppress or enslave our neighbors. But we neither love them like ourselves, nor even at all. For what does it mean for me to love my neighbor as myself?

I suppose that at the least it means that I will do him no harm, and at the most that I will allow no one else to do him any harm. It means that I will rejoice when he is happy, and that I will cry when he is hurt. It means that I will not be able to eat when he is hungry, or able to sleep when he is afflicted.

That is simple enough. But it is not easy. It is difficult—and, more than difficult, it is unnatural. For it is natural for man to love himself more than he loves his neighbor. It is natural for man to love his own children more than he loves his neighbor's children. Yet we need not be surprised that God requires of us something unnatural. For the kingdom he is preparing for us is not a supernatural kingdom. It is a kingdom where

> The wolf shall dwell with the lamb, and the leopard shall lie down with the kid, and the calf and the lion and the fatling tohgether, and a little child shall lead them. The cow and the bear shall feed; their young shall lie down together; and the lion shall eat straw like the ox. The suckling child shall play over the hole of the asp, and the weaned child shall put his hand in the adder's den. They shall not hurt or destroy in all my holy mountain; for the earth shall be full of the knowledge of the Lord as the waters cover the sea.

Now, this is obviously the description of a supernatural kingdom. For lions to lie down with lambs without the one eating the other will require a basic change in the nature of the beasts. Are we then doomed, mere natural men that we are, to do nothing about this kingdom until the creator of all beasts, in his own good time, shall decide to change the leopard's spots? Are we then destined to sit uselessly by, relieved of all responsibility, until the Day of Doom when the judge of us all shall cast down the mighty from their seat and the meek shall inherit the earth?

No, we do not believe that. We do not believe it or we would not have come to this place today. For we come here to proclaim boldly in the witness of all, "Thy kingdom come, thy will be done on earth as it is in heaven," and men of faith and courage do not say with their lips what they will not do with their lives. How then are we to redeem that pledge of prayer and praise? We cannot hold a plebiscite to elect a king for that kingdom, for it already has a king, and he is God himself. We cannot call a constitutional convention to draw up rights and duties for the citizens of that kingdom for its king has already established its laws. But we can behave like good citizens in that kingdom—and good citizens are simply those who obey the law.

Indeed, it is only because of our franchise in that kingdom, and only to the extent that we are good citizens of it, that we are able to do what we are going to do this morning. We are going to lay hands on one among us and set him apart and place on his shoulders the heavy burden we are unable or unwill ing to carry for ourselves—that is, to work fulltime, day and night, with his whole heart and total strength, to establish that kingdom in our midst.

Ignacio, my faithful student, my good friend, my Christian comrade, we, the people of God assembled in this place, the Body of Christ in this world, laity and clergy together, in the presence of our chief pastor, the Bishop, are going to set you apart for all time, and mark you so that you can never be unmarked, as Priest, Prophet, Preacher, and Healer. We charge you as Priest to sanctify the important passages in our lives—to baptize our children, to marry them when it is their time, to comfort them and us in our travails, and to bury us decently when it is our time. We charge you as Prophet to observe the historic events of the world about you and look for God's purpose in them, and when you discern it, to speak it out, and act. We charge you as Preacher to remind us at all times that if we love God with all our heart and all our soul and all our mind, we will see his kingdom, and to teach us in various and sundry ways how we may show forth our love for our neighbors as for ourselves. We charge you as Healer to pour balm on the sores of our sick society which cannot be healed by an act of congress or by presidential decree, and to bind up our wounds that cannot be healed by surgeon or pharmacist because we have inflicted them on ourselves.

These charges will require of you both service and leadership. You will quickly learn that service is not easy and leadership less easy still. For Christian men are hard to please and difficult to lead. Many of us are old and slow learners, and we will not quickly accept new ideas. Many of us are arrogant: we watched you growing up and we think we know more than you do. Many of us are selfish, and we will not gladly share goods with those who do not have them. Many of us are jealous, and we will be envious of your position, advantages, and salary. Many of us are petty, and we will rejoice in your sins because they will make our own seem lighter. But if you bear with us, we will show you that we love you, and we will learn that you love us, and in this way you will come into the Kingdom of Heaven.

May God the Father of all creation send you forth to split the hardened human heart so that the living waters of his compassion may flow forth therefrom.

May Jesus Christ the Good Shepherd send you forth as sheep among sheep, wolf among wolves, to reconcile together the mighty and the meek in his justice.

May God the Holy Spirit, pillar of fire by night and cloud by day, lead you forth to fan into tongues of flame the sparks of his love wherever you may find them, and where you do not, to scatter them.

BIBLIA Y CIENCIA, AMOR Y LIBERTAD

(Talk given in Our Lady of the Immaculate Concepcion Church, Batac, 1 September 1964.)

WE HAVE COME together here today to thank God for the gift to the Filipino people of the life and work, the death and victory, of the Most Reverend Dr. Gregorio Aglipay y Labayan.

I join this gathering with mixed feelings of shame and pride. I come before you humbly and with a sense of history, mindful of the fact that people of my race held your people in subjugation for many centuries, that citizens of my country destroyed the first Philippine Republic, and that members of my Church refused Gregorio Aglipay the friendship and comfort he asked for. I address you with humility in the presence of heroes of your Church who were fighting for religious freedom up and down this beautiful Ilocos coast before I was born, and of others who joined the same battle all over again just a few years ago in this very building. Here in this shrine, before the altar you have raised in the memory of Bishop Aglipay and in the presence of his last mortal remains, I have a sense of unimportance for having been born in a land where I could enjoy religious freedom without the least effort or sacrifice on my part.

Yet I come with a certain sense of pride, grateful for the honor of having been invited to participate in an intimate moment of worship in your Church family, for being the first American to serve your Church as missionary, and for having been appointed Director of a school bearing the proud name of the first Supreme Bishop of the Philippine Independent Church. As the Director of Aglipay Institute, I come not as a complete outsider nor a total stranger to the life and thoughts of the first Obispo Maximo.

Aglipay Institute's school motto is a quotation from the words of Monsignor Aglipay once to be found inscribed on many altars in Ilocandia: *Biblia y ciencia, amor y Libertad* ("Bible and science, love and liberty"). Any educator would note that Bishop Aglipay did not simply list these four terms—*Biblia, ciencia, amor y libertad*—but rather divided them into two pairs—Bible and science, love and liberty—and admire the deeper wisdom of the special alignment. We have all seen examples of the double folly of the unenlightened use of Scripture by the ignorant—the quotation of a word or sentence out of context on the one hand, or abject superstition on the other. All of us know only too well that we live in a world where all life could be snuffed out in a few minutes through the efforts of a science unenlightened by Divine Revelation. Just as the Bible and the sciences must go hand in hand, so, too, love and liberty dare not be separated, for love without liberty is selfishness, and liberty without love self-destroying chaos. Indeed, it is a mockery even to speak of love without liberty, for to love requires the freedom not to love: loyalty and worship acquired by force is not love. It was precisely this realization which led Gregorio Aglipay to fight not merely for the emancipation of his country in the political sense, but also for the religious freedom of the Filipino conscience.

Were it not for the life and work of patriots like Bishop Aglipay, we would not today be enjoying the political and religious freedom under which it is possible to operate a school bearing his name. It is therefore fitting that graduates of this school should be imbued with an abiding awareness of that four-fold motto which underlay its founding. Our youths must go forth with enough understanding of the Bible to realize their responsibility before God for the whole universe, and enough scientific knowledge to exercise stewardship over that environment; they must be committed to the love of all mankind and not just their friends and families, and willing to fight for liberty from tyranny of local loyalties and political parties. We are but a few gathered before this shrine today, but we represent an entire nation in our gratitude for the life of a great hero in the Philippine Revolution. Whether a member of the Philippine Independent Church, the Filipino Christian Church, the Episcopal Church, or the Iglesia ni Cristo, no Filipino need be ashamed to honor the memory of Gregorio Aglipay by marking his personal life with that password of "Bible and science, Love and liberty."

The late Obispo Maximo was in his lifetime a handsome man and a powerful man, and, I understand, he had that *amor propio* common to strong and handsome men. Would he not have been proud to be with us today, twenty-five years later, and see the honor and dignity of that nation for whose birthright he fought so hard? How proud he would be to see Filipino statesmen sitting in the councils of the nations of the world and casting equal votes with their former oppressors! How proud he would be to see a Filipino general presiding over the United Nations Organization assembled!

And would he not also be proud of his Church? We are too often given to speaking of the Iglesia Filipina Independiente as a weak and poor church in the midst of rich and powerful enemies; we forget that it has attained a triumphant stature in the eyes of international Christendom of which Bishop Aglipay could hardly have dreamed. The concordats of intercommunion which have seated bishops of the Philippine Independent Church in mutual respect and honor beside the bishops and metropolitans of some of the oldest churches of five continents could not even have been thought of fifty years ago. When Gregorio Aglipay was a young Roman Catholic cleric, the only kind of relations a Filipino priest could have expected abroad were those of surrender and submission. Surely he would be as astounded as he would be proud to see his successor in cordial private audience with a Roman cardinal, to see him standing beside the Archbishop of Canterbury in the Cathedral of St. Paul in London, intoning a consecration prayer in the Pilipino tongue at the elevation of an Anglican priest to the episcopate!

I hope it does not overstep the bounds of modesty to suggest that he might not have been displeased, either, to see an educational institution bearing his name under the direction of a foreigner who came not as a landlord or tax collector but as the humble servant of a Filipino Church, not supported by the power of an alien army but at the invitation of a Filipino board of directors, and not in the name of an Italian prince, but in love of Christ.

THE SPIRIT OF GREGORIO AGLIPAY

(Message delivered during the 34th Aglipay Annual Death Anniversary Celebration in the Cultural Center of Batac Municipality, Ilocos Norte, on 17 September 1974.)

I HAVE had the temerity to accept the undeserved honor of your invitation to deliver a short message on the life of Monsignor Dr. Gregorio Aglipay y Labayan, first Obispo Maximo of the Iglesia Filipina Independiente.

I consider it part of my message to begin with an apology. I wish to apologize for addressing you in a foreign language. Your ability to receive my little message in my own tongue is a tribute to the talent of the Filipino people, and I congratulate you for it. Your willingness to do so is a tribute to the hospitality of the Filipino people, and I thank you for it. Indeed, your willingness to receive me here at all, alien that I am, on this most intimate occasion of national sentiment, can only be explained by what we Americans call Filipino big-heartedness.

Now, big-heartedness is a good thing for making love or writing poetry, but in actual fact, enlargement of the heart is a disease. It is a debilitating disease which leaves its victims prostrate and dependent on the ministrations of other people outside themselves. Perhaps this was the sickness, or part of the sickness, which the sixth President of the second Republic had in mind when, two years ago, he said we were living in a sick society. When a society is sick, it is not suffering from a physical ailment that can be cured by medicine purchased in the *botica*. When a society gets sick, it suffers from spiritual sickness, and therefore it takes a spiritual medicine to cure it. I wish to suggest that the proper medicine in the present case is the spirit of Gregorio Aglipay.

Of course, it is difficult to find a man's spirit, and especially difficult in the case of Gregorio Aglipay. For when we consult history books on the shelves of libraries, we only learn the cold facts of his life, and these cold facts do not disclose his spirit.

We read, for example, that Gregorio Aglipay was not a scholar. Even the facts of his school days are cited to further the contention: he got poor grades in the seminary and in his examination for the priesthood. But his spirit escapes these facts. The facts do not reveal the conditions in the old Vigan seminary where all the desks and books and subjects and professors and ideas were foreign, and everything Filipino was wrong or inferior or at least in need of correction. The facts do not disclose the galling frustration of being a Filipino patriot and dreaming of the Filipino future under such circumstances. For it is from the anguish of such a situation, not from textbooks or classroom exercises, that the yearning for dignity and justice and independence is born.

It is said that Gregorio Aglipay was no saint. Certainly Gregorio Aglipay never claimed to be a saint, and probably he never dreamed of becoming one. Professor Teodoro A. Agoncillo, dean of historians of the Filipino people, and my mentor and colleague, says: "Aglipay was no saint; he was a man, a human being, a Filipino"—and, he might have added, an Ilocos Norteano and a Bataqueno. The heroes of the Ilocos are not known for their piety and sanctimoniousness; they are known for their valor and *amor propio*. Dr. Ruben Santos-Cuyugan, Chancellor of the Philippine Center for Advanced Studies, an autonomous unit of the University of the Philippines recently created by presidential decree, was quoted in an interview as saying the Center needed men "with a certain fanaticism for the nation." Certainly Gregorio Aglipay was such a man. But the isolated facts of his life might not reveal it.

Gregorio Aglipay was no theologian. So the facts recorded in history books tell us. For forty years he wandered in the desert, cut off from other Christian bodies, apparently drifting from one theological position to another. But if he wandered in such a wilderness, he was driven there. He was driven there by his unwillingness to submit to a Roman Church in which Filipinos could not determine their own destiny, and by the unwillingness of American Protestants to accept him for what he was. And if he was searching in that desert, he was searching for a theology and a church that would best serve the needs of the Filipino people. The watchword of his search was nothing any theologian ever said, but "What does Christ say to the Filipino people?" But no history book records this spirit.

No, Gregorio Aglipay was not a scholar, not a saint, nor a theologian. He was a prophet.

Now, a prophet is a man who feels fiercely. He feels fiercely about the injustices of the world in which he lives, and out of the anguish which he suffers in that world comes the vision, under God, of a better world. Aglipay the Prophet lived out his whole mortal life in such a world, for in the flesh he never tasted the fruits of his vision—an independent Filipino nation enrolled in the family of nations, and an independent Filipino church in communion with worldwide Christendom. Such a nation and such a church—of the

Filipino people, *by* the Filipino people, and *for* the Filipino people—that was the spirit of Gregorio Aglipay!

And so my message to you this morning is simply this: what the New Society needs is the spirit of Gregorio Aglipay. That spirit has been bequeathed to you Filipinos, Ilocos Norteanos and Bataquenos like a living flame. I pray God grant you the wisdom, the patience, and the courage never to be distracted by any lesser spirit from the awesome responsibility which has been given you as Keepers of the Flame.

CHURCHES OF SILENCE

(Commencement address, St. Andrew's Theological Seminary, 13 March 1976.)

LAST YEAR I had the privilege of attending your graduation exercises in this chapel and hearing the inspiring and timely commencement address of Dr. Salvador P. Lopez, former President of the University of the Philippines, on the subject of "Influencing Today's Revolution." You will recall that his message was that it was every Filipino's duty to try to influence that revolution by expressing his opinions of it in such a way that they might reach, and perhaps influence, the President who is the author of the revolution. He closed with the direct charge:

> Members of the graduating class: this, then, is your responsibility—this is the task cut out for you—to go forth among the people and preach constantly that not only their individual redemption but also the redemption of their country lies in the hollow of their hands.

I don't know how many members of that graduating glass—or this graduating class—took Dr. Lopez's advice. But many Filipinos did. His words received wide circulation in periodicals not owned or controlled by the government, and many of his readers—supreme court justices among them—considered them to be his most important words written in his finest hour. And, whether there was any connection or not, before the year was out, Manila saw an example of the results that could be produced by acting upon just such advice.

On November 3, 1975, President Marcos issued Presidential Decree 823, which stated that "all forms of strikes, picketing and lockouts are hereby strictly prohibited" and that "any person violating this Decree shall forthwith be arrested and taken into custody for the duration of the national emergency." A few days later, his Eminence, Jaime L. Sin, Archbishop of Manila, addressed a letter of protest to the President and ordered it read aloud from every Roman Catholic pulpit in the land. The Hon. Jose B. L. Reyes, former Chief Justice of the Supreme Court and past president of the Integrated Bar of the Philippines, produced and publicized a protest written from the standpoint of a jurist, and Secretary of Labor Blas Ople accepted an invitation from the Cosmopolitan Church to discuss the Decree in an open forum of Christian critics. The *Philippine Collegian,* official organ of the student body of the state university, put out a thought-provoking editorial which sparked two weeks of almost daily symposia and convocations attended not only by students but by workers, religious and prominent Filipino nationalists. Just last week, a waiter in a restaurant where I was eating told me he had attended one of these meetings, and when I asked if he were a working student, he said, "No, but how can a waiter find out what's going on in the country if he just stays in the restaurant?"

Finallly, on December 6, thousands of workers, nuns, priests, students, seminarians and laymen gathered together for an ecumenical service in the parish church of Our Lady of San Loreto in Bustillos, Sampaloc, and then processed in the direction of Malacanang Palace. They were stopped before reaching Mendiola Bridge, so they proceeded in procession to Plaza Miranda instead, gathering thousands of other Filipino citizens along the way, and there they spent the evening expressing their opinions and praying. And, just as Dr. Lopez had envisioned, the President heard their protests and before Christmas Day amended Presidential Decree 823 by issuing a new presidential decree, No. 851.

I do not tell this story for the purpose of either approving or disapproving the stand taken by the various actors who participated in it. As an alien in your midst, I have no political personality, nor do I enjoy all the civil rights guaranteed to you by your several constitutions. I tell the story simply to set the background for a personal experience I had during that time. It happened that I met a former student of mine, one of the best students I had ever taught, now making good use of his education to earn a living for himself and his wife and family here in this greater Manilan metropolis. In the course of our conversation, he happened to ask me what time it was. And after I told him, he said: "You know, Scotty, I always remember how you taught us twenty years ago that the correct expression is, 'What time is it?' and not 'What is your time?' and ever since then when I hear some important Filipino with a fancy American degree ask, 'What is your time?' I am thankful that you were my teacher."

In the course of the same conversation I also discovered that he had never heard of Presidential Decree 823.

And the impact of that discovery stripped me suddenly naked and exposed to the gaze of the Creator who had called me to the profession of missionary and schoolteacher in the first place. For the question was unavoidable: had I been true to that calling by producing students who prided themselves on a command of foreign grammar which set them apart from their fellow Filipinos but could not even notice what was happening to their fellow men? And if I had not, how had I failed?

The answer was all too obvious. I had failed, and I had failed because I had lived in such a way that grammar seemed more important than love.

And yet, my life has not been a complete failure. To teach other men to speak a foreign language is not a totally insignificant accomplishment. It is as if I had lived my life in two separate compartments, in the one of which I had been successful, and in the other a failure. It is sobering to think that a man could live his life in two such contradictory ways, and it is more sobering still to wonder if success in the one was not in direct proportion to failure in the other—that is, the suspicion that the more punctually my classes met, the more disciplined my students became, and the more efficiently I laid down the rules of English grammar, the less the light of Christ shone through me.

I would not have burdened you with this maudlin little confession if I had thought my case was unique or unusual. But I do not. Rather, I think it is typical of the educational system I serve and the society in which I live. The state university might provide a grander example of just such a contradiction as I seem to have suffered in my personal career. On the one hand, it is supported by the sweat of the Filipino people's labor and therefore exists only to serve them, and so it aims to produce public-spirited, civic-minded men and women conscious of the responsibility which their privileged status entails and willing to dedicate their skills to the service of their fellow men rather than to the advancement of their own careers and the prosperity of their own fortunes. And yet, on the other hand, most of its students are in actual fact motivated by the desire to get good jobs in a land where jobs, good or bad, are scarce, and to accumulate for themselves a disproportionate share of the world's goods in a world where the goods are limited. Long before they become seniors they learn that the society into which they will graduate will not reward them for the ideals with which they were imbued as freshmen, but for the skills they can offer for sale.

But is it really necessary to have such a schizophrenic educational system? Would it not be possible to design an institution of higher learning which could produce, let us say, an engineer competent both to build bridges and to do so for the common good—or even a missionary who could teach the love of Christ and English grammar both?

As a matter of fact, this is precisely the goal of the educational system of one of our neighboring states. In the People's Republic of China, a nation the President of our own Republic has called the leader of the Third World, educational strategists speak in terms of producing graduates who are "red and expert." By "expert" they mean having the skills to design railroads or improve agriculture or cure diseases. And by "red" they mean having an attitude which sees these skills as a form of service to the common people, and the common people as the object of their service and thus the very reason for their existence in the first place. A friend of mine who works for the World Health Organization attended an international conference of doctors not so long ago in which some Chinese colleagues who were products of that educational system read a paper on some medical research which was a real contribution to the advancement of medical science. These were circumstances in which doctors produced by our educational system would have been proud to read a paper in order to enhance their professional reputation, win promotions, and increase their income. But these Chinese doctors were obviously uncomfortable with the attention they were attracting, and embarrassed by the implication of individual praise which excluded the hundreds and thousands of other Chinese whose teamwork had made the report possible. This, I take it, is what is meant by "red and expert."

I wonder if we could not develop our own equivalent of this red-and-expert condition which seems to produce such happy results. Perhaps "white and expert"? Or no—"white" is not a very auspicious term, is it? In comparison with red, it seems to suggest timidity and sterility, and in the twentieth-century heraldry of international politics symbolizes the forces of reaction and oppression. How about "green"—"green and expert"—as the educational goal of a Christian republic? For green is the color of verdure and youth, of growth and hope. It is typified by the seedling which, when dropped in the crack in the rock, belies its delicate appearance by growing up to split the rock. It is the color of the grass which covers all, springing back to life again no matter how often it is mowed down, the cogon which survives all burnings. And it is the color appropriate to a Creator God who brings forth living waters in the sandy desert, and makes the barren places bloom as the barren woman fruitful with child.

But how will we begin?

Well, we might seek a clue in that neighboring state. Now that diplomatic relations have been established between our two nations, we might send over a fact-finding committee in the guise of a cultural exchange to ferret out the secret. And if we did, I think I know what they would come back and tell us. The secret of that red-and-expertness, they would say, is simply this: they have a Prophet of Redness living in their midst. They just study his words, master his ideas, and follow his leadership. So the solution for us would appear to be simple, too. We need only find the Prophet of Greenness in our midst, listen to what he says, and love and obey him.

But it is right here that the analogy breaks down. For we have no Prophet of Greenness in our midst, nor will we ever have. For the greenness of which we speak is already planted like a seed in the inner core of being of every living thing. It can be nourished and developed where it already exists, but it cannot be injected by any discipline or indoctrination where it does not. It does not respond to any leadership dinned into the consciousness by loudspeakers and mass media, but to that which speaks in a still, small voice in the midst of storm. Its laws are not promulgated on public walls in large character posters, but engraved directly on the stony parts of the heart, there to be grown over by flesh lusting after life. For in the human animal, this greenness is called *conscience*.

But if we can find no Prophet of that greenness, we can at least find examples of men who were green and expert. We need look no deeper into history than our own colonial past for examples.

The Philippines was once dominated by several orders of friars who were expert in the practice of their profession and in implementing the goals of the Spanish King, and, in many cases, green enough in conscience to recognize the sinful nature of the King's servants in the field and do something about it. When these friars accompanied troops into battle, they were expected not merely to administer sacraments and succor the wounded, but to prevent needless bloodshed and show mercy on captives. When Filipino forces who had submitted to Spanish rule were led out against their independent brothers who had not, their leaders were often friar captains who hoped to prevent atrocities of vengeance and the wanton destruction of whole villages and towns. And in areas of frontier feuds, such friars were known to report commanders who deliberately prolonged hostilities lest the restoration of peace deprive them of the advantages they enjoyed through military occupation. As *protectores de los indios,* they even committed acts of civil disobedience to sabotage exploitation of their flocks. During the Dutch wars, some friars in Pangasinan set fire to a forest to prevent further hardship at forced labor in timber-cutting and ship-building, and two centuries later their comrades of the cloth protested the cruelties of the Tobacco Monopoly by openly smoking contraband tobacco and encouraging their Filipino parishioners to do the same.

As an historian, I look with some awe at the courage of these conscience-stricken clergy, green and expert as they were in a state where it was easy to be misunderstood and even archbishops and governors general could die in chains for having touched some raw nerve in the colonial body politic. As a layman, it is probably presumptuous for me even to mention so sensitive a subject to future clergymen just about to test their own courage on the cutting edge of the Church's conscience. Yet the history of the Church has not been wanting for examples of other laymen who presumed not only to criticize the clergy conscience but to influence it by the example of their own actions.

When John Milton wrote the greatest epic in the English language, he stated that his purpose was to justify the ways of God to man, and the ways of man to God. The basis for this lofty presumption was not mere scholarship or literary elegance, but a lifetime of courageous obedience to a Christian conscience in a day when the affairs of Church and State were dangerously intertwined. He lived in a time of insurrection, rebellion, and civil war which overthrew a government, beheaded a king, and established a dictatorship. He was himself an elite *ilustrado* with a private income and the shoulder-length hair of a Renaissance aristocrat, but he took the side of the commoners against the monarchy out of religious conviction, and the Puritan cause against the Anglican Church which supported that monarchy. The bulk of all his writing, both prose and verse, was inspired by and dedicated to a Christian cause, not least those polemic pamphlets against the King which made Milton personal secretary to the head of the rebel state, and his pen the sharpest sword on the rebel side.

I am afraid that had I been living in Milton's day, I would have been on the other side. As a law-abiding citizen, I would probably not have been attracted to a revolution that aimed to unseat a reigning monarch, no matter how tyrannical. As a member of the Anglican Communion, I would probably not have questioned the leadership of my bishops who supported the establishment that supported them. And as a timid and peaceable man, I would probably not have had the courage to risk detention and death as Milton did even if I had agreed with him.

Yet it is the strange fact that it was the voice of Milton speaking across three centuries which influenced my life more than any other one voice. For it was while reading a certain passage out of John Milton that I decided to become a missionary and a schoolteacher. When I first read that passage, I could not go on, so I went back and read it a second time. And then I looked up from the printed page and knew right then, in that moment, what my calling was. I knew that what I wanted more than anything else was to serve my Church by raising my voice with tongue or pen on her behalf when she had need. And she has need now. May I therefore share those words of Milton with you?

> For me, I have determined to lay up as the best treasure and solace of a good old age, if God vouchsafe it me, the honest liberty of free speech from my youth, where I shall think it available in so dear a concernment as the church's good. For if I be, either by disposition or what other cause, too inquisitive or suspicious of myself and mine own doings, who can help it? But this I foresee, that should the church be brought under heavy oppression, and God have given me ability the while to reason against the man that should be the author of so foul a deed, or should she, by blessing from above

or the industry and courage of faithful men, change this her distracted estate into better days without the least furtherance or contribution of these few talents which God at that present had lent me, I foresee what stories I should hear within myself, all my life after, of discourage and reproach.

Timorous and ungrateful, the church of God is again at the foot of her insulting enemies, and thou bewailest. What matters it thee, or thy bewailing? When time was, thou couldst not find a syllable of all that thou hadst read or studied, to utter on her behalf. Yet case and leisure was given thee for thy retired thoughts out of the sweat of other men. Thou hadst the diligence, the parts, the language of a man, if a vain cause were to be adorned or beautified, but when the cause of God and his church was to be pleaded, for which purpose that tongue was given thee which thou hast, God listened if he could hear thy voice among his zealous servants, but thou wert dumb as a beast. From henceforward, be that which thine own brutish silence hath made thee.

The Quakers have a saying, "There are many voices in the world: some speak to some men, and some speak to others." Milton's voice speaks to me. I don't know whether it speaks to you or not. But it easily might. For we and our churches live in a time of national crisis and testing of faith just as Milton and his church did. Our two churches, like his church, are young and insecure, and therefore so concerned with their own growth and survival they do not care to read the signs of the times. They are poor and anxious, and therefore hanker after treasures corruptible by moth and rust and liable to theft in the night. They are small and weak, and therefore tempted to close their eyes to large problems and their hearts to large needs. And they are minority churches full of minority peoples, and therefore inclined to ignore, or exploit, the politics of the majority. Would that some Milton were living at this hour when we so fondly speak of the separation of Church and State, to tell us from his own experience that the affairs of God and the affairs of men can never be separated. What questions might he not ask to test the corporate conscience of our two churches?

Are our preachers in their pulpits constantly exhorting us to find Christlike answers to the questions posed by our national emergency; do they ask us each what Christ requires of us in time of crisis? Are our pastors in their parishes leading us out to discover those robber bands who inflict the wounds on wayfarers we good Samaritans so love to bind up; do they condemn our charity when it is the opiate of the guilty? Are our priests daily at their altars praying for the repose of the souls of our sons and students dying in the field of battle; do they sanctify these sacrifices for the security of our New Society by public prayer? Are our chaplains present in the midst of war, turning the edge of vengeance and staying the executioner's hand; do they handle prisoners as Christ would deal with his enemies? Are our bishops standing firmly behind our governors and commanders, looking over their shoulders with love as they make the decisions which affect the lives of a whole nation of God's people; do they speak in their ears the voice of prophecy and Godly counsel?

I do not know the answer to these questions because no survey has been made of so private a part of our churches' lives. But this I fear: that should these lives, insofar as we can see them in public, be weighed together in the balances of God's own justice, they would be found wanting. For the Philippine Independent Church and the Philippine Episcopal Church today are churches characterized not by bringing good tidings to the afflicted and binding up the broken- hearted, not by proclaiming liberty to captives and the opening of prisons to those who are bound, and not by proclaiming the year of the Lord's favor and the day of the vengeance of our God—but by silence.

I realize that these are grim words with which to conclude an address on so victorious an occasion as the commencement of your professional careers after your academic preparations. Perhaps their burden can be lightened by the reflection that they are, after all, only one man's opinion, and that all men are fallible, some of us more than others. I assure you there is no man among you who would rather that they were wrong than I. Moreover, you have the choice to disbelieve them. Indeed, you have the choice not only to disbelieve them, but to deny them, and not only to deny them, but to disprove them. For it is within your power to demonstrate that my accusations are unfair, unwarranted, or untrue. By the lives you live and the ministry you follow, you can show that your church is not the subject of the picture I have just painted. Therefore I throw this challenge to you this morning, Filipino youth—

Go forth from this place and by the practice of your priesthood, by the passion of your preaching, and by the power of your prophecy, *make my words false!*

OTHER BOOKS AUTHORED OR EDITED BY
WILLIAM HENRY SCOTT
Published by New Day Publishers

Chips
Cracks in the Parchment Curtain
Discovery of the Igorots
Hollow Ships on a Wine-Dark Sea
Ilocano Responses to American Aggression, 1900-1901
Prehispanic Source Materials for the Study of Philippine History
A Sagada Reader